A Foreword by SARK

Dear Deluxe Reader,

Each poem story in Kelly's book is like a thought puddle splashing out from the Ocean of Love. Refreshing. Tangy. Soothing. Surprising.

This book instantly cuts through the worried, wounded voices in your head, and connects you to your deepest self—the part of you that knows that beneath it all lies an endless sea of supportive, caring power.

There is truth here served like crispy, sweet layers of honey pistachio baklava warm from the oven.

As you experience this book, your inner child may come out to skip, climb a tree, jump rope, and sing . . . or maybe she feels abandoned right now and just needs you to brush her hair, spoon her some homemade soup, and then dress her in some clean play clothes when she is ready . . .

Perhaps you will encounter multiple inner children and other overlooked characters. You realize they need your embrace and recognition. As Walt Whitman said, "We contain multitudes."

Kelly acknowledges the emotional journey, the ache, the innate awkwardness that comes with being a human being. She also reminds us we have the power to choose each moment to see things differently. To believe that every dark path winds its way to timeless hope.

So get out your art pencils and color the whimsical illustrations that fill every page of this book—including twenty coloring pages you can frame and share. Solve puzzles and dive deeper into your soul with the play pages at the end of this book.

The creative process goes something like this:
1. Wow, I have a great idea!
2. Oh, it's all been said before.
3. Others say it better.
4. People will reject me for expressing this. I feel too vulnerable.
5. It's junk.
6. Maybe there's some value in it.
7. Maybe my unique flavor will add to the collection of guideposts to awakening.
8. I do feel inspired.
9. I'll go with my heart and risk it!
10. I'll do it no matter what ups and downs I encounter!

Kelly decided to risk it~

She felt the twitter bugs exploding inside her—fireflies, shooting stars, rays of light that she couldn't hold inside anymore. They woke her up early in the morning to create with colorful pens on huge unlined newsprint paper. Her muse brought the lilting rhymes to her. Her hand swirled and her heart soared as inspiration poured through her.

And Kelly has three more books of poems already written, waiting to be surrounded by the intricate charm of Lee Kaster's pen. I look forward to much more from her! Let's honor the power of authenticity. Let's be part of the connection that Kelly so vividly brings alive in these pages.

Let your true, ageless, unflappable being rise up. Let's realize the parasitic inner critic/ego/pain body is not the real you. Let's party with Kelly!

—SARK   author/artist/creative fountain
PlanetSARK.com

"A wonderful juicy creation, exploding with life, energy, joy and inspiration, to enliven the soul and jazz the spirit of readers young and old. Enjoy this gift of the heart, and give a copy to someone you love."

—Eliezer Sobel, author of **The 99th Monkey** and **Blue Sky, White Clouds**

"Equal parts poetry, coloring mandala, and meditative journal, **Wild Dancing Heart** is a must for any reflective soul. Grab your imagination and colored pencils for a spiritual and literary journey!"

—Jennifer Ozgur, author of **One Million Kisses**

"**Wild Dancing Heart** dives into the human spirit with a fun, lighthearted tone and a deep understanding of life's challenges. I highly recommend this amazing little jewel."

—Allyson Roberts, author / talk show host of **Outrageous Freedom**

"I LOVE your book and the whimsical illustrations—makes my heart happy! Thank you for bringing such a lovely book into the world.
Wild Dancing Heart is a delightful romp into your soul. This book can be opened randomly for a bit of inspiration. Break out your pencil, crayons, or felt pens to color in some of the pages and the messages will speak to you on a deeper level. Like a Sherpa guiding your path with sage advice, **Wild Dancing Heart** will take you on an uplifting journey which is sure to delight your spirit!"
—Violette Clark, author/artist of
Journal Bliss

"Kelly Athena's poetry will uplift and delight your spirit. It has a magical quality that heals the mind and helps us all to see the value of Life and our own Being. You will find peace and joy in her work!"
—Alexandria Stevens, author of
Power Tools: Idea You Can Use To Disassemble Fear

Wild dancing Heart

Kelly Athena

art by Lee Kaster

Copyright © Kelly Athena 2017
All Rights Reserved.

ISBN-10: 0-9847935-1-8
ISBN-13: 978-0-9847935-1-8
Library of Congress Control Number 2016959071

1. Poetry /Women Authors
2. Art & Photography / Drawing / Coloring Books for Grown-ups

Wild Dancing Heart is available at special quantity discounts to you or your company, educational institution, charity, or writing organization for educational purposes, fund-raising campaigns, reselling, subscription incentives, sales promotions, or gifts.
For more information, please contact Publisher@PurpleCatPublishing.com

Cover and interior Art and Design by Lee Kaster

PurpleCatPublishing.com

PHOENIX, ARIZONA USA

This book is an invitation
for your
Timeless Inner Child
to come out and play!

Look for a musical note
like this

hidden in each poem

Acknowledgments

Thank you to my family, friends, and tribe of online supporters for cheering me on in this endeavor.

Thanks to my mom, Val, for her lifelong encouragement of my creativity, and her example of persistence and hope.

Thanks to my late father, Sam Parnum, for filling my childhood with the love of nature and music.

Thanks to my sister, Jamie, for showing me the beauty of creativity through her dance and choreography.

Thanks to Caci Chapel, Hali Fields, Randa Hightower, Alex Stevens, and Paula Watkins, for their friendship and assistance in the editing process.

Thanks to the many authors and teachers who have inspired me: Rumi, Julia Cameron, Eckhart Tolle, Kathleen Killen, my third grade teacher, Sue Monk Kidd, Kahlil Gibran, Crockett Johnson, Joseph Dillard, Marianne Williamson, Florence Scovel Shinn, Edward Abbey, Robert A. Johnson, and Jerry Ruhl to name just a few.

Thanks to Crista Aldridge for creating the heart puzzle and word scrambles using words and phrases from this book.

Special thanks to Jackson for always seeing the best in me.

And an ocean full of thanks to Lee Kaster, the marvelous artist who brought these poems alive with her intricate, playful artwork.

TABLE OF CONTENTS

Suggested Uses for this Book 1
Alphabet of Authenticity 2
Alone 4
Attraction 6
Authentic 8
Beautiful 10
Clues 12
The Deeper You 14
Doormat's Declaration 16
Equations 18
Flower Power 20
Flutter 22
Freedom 24
Friends 26
Give Me A Break 28
Got Hate? 30
Guidepost 32
Inner Journey 34
In This I Trust 36
Jolt 38
Let Love Grow 40
Mermaid 44
Mirrors 46
My Agenda 48
Perception 50
Promise 52
Question 54

Reflection 58
Relationships 60
Remarkable 62
Right Now 64
Shell Dweller 66
Soul Scribbles 68
Spilling Out 70
Spun 74
Star Child 76
Success 80
Surrounded 82
The Power of Friendship 84
The Power of Joy 86
The Wisdom of a Rose 88
To Be a Bird 90
Who You Are 92
Who Am I? 94
Wild Dancing Heart 96
You and Me 98
Zesty 100
For Coloring and Sharing 103
Heart Puzzle 144
Word Search I 146
Word Search II 148
Heart Puzzle Answers 150
Word Search Answers 152
Getting Deeper 157
Meet The Author 166
Meet The Artist 168

Wild Dancing Heart

Suggested Uses For This Book

Use the poems as prompts for your own writing: Read a poem and then write about the words or phrases that pop into your mind.

Treat this collection as a personalized messenger service: Flip open the book to a random page and see what message is waiting there for you. Suggest this book to your book club or start your own *Wild Dancing Heart* Book Club.

Read a poem at special occasions, such as birthdays Mother's Day, New Year's Eve, or even a funeral.

As an experiment, take turns reading a poem to your partner each night before going to sleep. See if it calms and brightens up your relationship.

Act out a poem with passion, drama, and props as you read it — then ask a friend to act one out. This can be quite cheering and possibly hilarious. Handy for when you can't think of what to say while visiting a friend in the hospital.

Ideal gift book for occasions such as birthdays, Valentine's Day, graduation, get well wishes, Mother's Day, Father's Day, Hanukkah, holidays and Christmas.

Many of the poems make delightful children's bedtime readings.

Kelly Athena

Alphabet of Authenticity

Abandon convention
Be your own best friend
Create constantly
Doubt the norm
Ease up
Free the multitudes that lie within
Grandly unfurl
Honor who you are
Ignite your intuition
Joy is your juice
Kindness rules
Laugh loud and long
Marry yourself first
Now is all you need
Open to the ocean of your possibilities
Play passionately
Quote the quietness
Research your radiance
Savor the sauce of your soul
Taste truth
Untame your uniqueness
Vibrate vividly
Well up with wisdom
Xpand exponentially
You are enough
Zero regrets

Kelly Athena

Someone pushed me into a corner
   of a musty dark attic
      where I lay curled up, unsure,
         stiff as an unlit candlewick.

They left a long time ago,
   tip-tapping down the staircase
   and shutting the door behind.
      I could have left here too
         so many times
   but I just stay in my mind
      and dream of flying away.

There's a crack in the window
 and I hear the curling branch of an oak
    tip-tapping on the glass
       tapping for me I think
          as if to say,

"Climb down my strong arms.
   It's okay to come play
      on my swing today,
         to arch in the glow of the sun,
            to blow the heavy dust away.
               We really could
                  have fun!"

Kelly Athena

ATTRACTION

I am
a **powerful** magnet
What I keep picturing,
I'll get

Whether a secret
or a well-known fact
What I focus on,
I'll attract

Whatever I'm feeling
strongest about
will **come to me**
without a doubt

If I see it
inside repeatedly
It will show up outside
it's a guarantee

Kelly Athena

Authentic

The pressure to conform
shoulders back, belly in
is like having to perform
and ignore what's
within:
My heart urging me
in a gentle voice
to stop and look inside
and make my own
choice

Wild Dancing Heart

So what if I'm a flop?
It's better to be free
than swap my soul so easily
This doesn't mean I won't cooperate
for a common cause
that's good and right
It just means I won't be suffocated
and relinquish what brings me
the most delight

So all the rigid creeds
and condescending critics
can gather dust
at the back of the shelf
The only one
I need approval from
is my Authentic Self

Kelly Athena

CLUES

In a cobweb
a diamond of
glistening dew

In a leaf
a parallel universe **clue**

In a finger
a **maze** of swirling curves

In a thought
The things that rule
your world

Wild Dancing Heart

the deeper you

You are a sphere of energy
within a greater
energy sphere
Though you appear
as a human being
it's only light
that I am seeing
You are in and through
and out of form
You will never die
you were always born

Kelly Athena

doormat's declaration of Freedom

Wild Dancing Heart — 16

I feel abused
when my views
are not **listened to**
but squashed like bugs
on the windshield
of your **mind**

I will **no longer**
waste my time
with someone who
is **not** kind

Find **another** doormat
to wipe your feet on today
'cause this one
has **stood up**
and
is walking **away!**

Kelly Athena

Shoulds = Expectations

Expectations = Disappointment

Disappointment = Resentment

Acceptance = Growth

Growth = Freedom

Freedom = Power

Power = Joy

Flower Power

The flower lost its perfect shape

"It's such an awful shame," they said

It went to seed, they called it dead

But did it lose **or did it win**

by **giving all** it had within?

Wild Dancing Heart

It rose again a hundred-fold
and spread across the landscape bold
in rainbow beauty blues and reds
it fanned through fields and riverbeds
to gardens, towns, and streams it led
while butterflies and bees were fed

All because
its petals
shed
All because
it lost its head

Kelly Athena

FLUTTER

My thoughts are jumbled,
   caught and torn
   twisted, stunted, stretched,
      half-born
   ever moving, never complete
      pounding like
         a bass drumbeat

So I pause
   and step back from everything
I stop and feel
   a flutter of wings
deep in the pit
   where I hold onto things

It's hope rising high
   like a dove from her nest

straight for the sky
on a sunlit quest
to a distant point with a boundless view
where all of life
looks sweet and new
Far beyond the endless chatter
to a place where nothing
really matters
beyond the knotted threads that bind
to the unfolding delight
of my design.

Kelly Athena

You are the universe

No need to rehearse

Jump out of your chair

Tuck flowers in your hair

Leap high in the air

with dazzle and flair

Soar like a bird

that has never heard

the word "no"

Just let go!

Kelly Athena

friends

A friend
is like a trellis
where I can climb,
grow and flourish,
and be in my prime

A friend is like a park
where it's fun to play
I'm never ridiculed
or chased away

A friend is like
the bright sun in the sky
shining full blast
though I laugh or cry

A friend is like having
a gentle massage
kneading out the knots
of self-sabotage

A friend is like snuggling
in a down comforter
making me feel warm,
safe and sure

A friend is like an angel
without the wings
where I can say
and do anything

A friend is like
a bottomless ocean of love
a shooting star
streaking down from above

So thank you for being
such a good friend
I'll love you always
there is no end

Kelly Athena

give me a break

I am a strict taskmaster
I must get
more done
faster
It's a recipe
for disaster
I forecast
a headache
up ahead

Time to take a break instead
Shake off this overwhelming dread
Catch a snowflake on my tongue
Remember all the songs I've sung
and all the flowers that have sprung
from seeds planted with my hands

I'll dissolve
harsh reprimanding
into gentle
understanding
After all, life
is about expanding
Not doing more
and keeping score
but taking time
to explore

Love is my only assignment
Peace my only alignment
To fear's offer I decline

Kelly Athena

Got hate? Go create.
Burning rage? Write a page.
Got complaints? Splash some paints.
Feel depressed? Go express.
Broken heart? Do some art!

Kelly Athena

GUIDEPOST

Let joy be your guidepost

Do what you cherish most

Savor and luxuriate

Quit doing things

that you hate

Kelly Athena

Inner Journey

Thoughts rush in at a blinding pace
How did I ever choose this place
of judge and jury, wild hurry
victim's story, constant worry
There is no prize for such a race
but blurry eyes
and drooping face

So I take a breath
slow, deep and long
Its rhythmic pulse
becomes a song
leading to a hidden gate
deep beyond my guilty weight

I find the key
 beneath a stone
of moss and cold and used up bone
 I turn the lock and swing the door
 and find within my central core
 a soothing stream so cool and wide
 it absorbs all I feel inside

 No more effort needed here
  where everything is calm and clear
 I dive in and let my body go
  with the steady pulling flow

I'm blasted out into the fall,
 suspended in a liquid wall
With closed eyes I'm finally seeing
 the spacious wonder of my being
where all is still
 all is bliss
 and I accept life's gentle kiss

Kelly Athena

in this i trust

In a hundred years
my body will be dust
and what possessed it will be poured out
into love's all-consuming roar
I will spin and swirl til I combust
and glitter out from every star
In this I trust
In this I trust

I'll still be close though I am far
as close as the teardrops that you cry
as close as the stardust in your eyes
I will be in your every breath
for there is no such thing as death
That was just a fairy tale
made up to keep you feeling frail

Wild Dancing Heart

Drum, dear heartbeat,
I am there
Breathe in and out, I'm in the air
Soar with me in lively dreams
for love's bonds cannot ever rust
Hope is supreme
Love is robust

In this I trust
In this I trust

Kelly Athena

JOLT

What kind of courage
would it take
to jolt awake
watch feelings surge
and truth emerge
To let your heart
cry and shake
shatter and skate
right off the ledge
where it was kept
way out of sight
to be polite

Go past the edges
of the box
where everything stays
so orderly
until you feel
the raindrops pelt you
scatter and melt you
into the sea
where you could finally
roll off the shelf
and ride the tide
of your
true self

Kelly Athena

Let Love Grow

Not just in fields
of straight neat rows
Not just like lawns
you have to mow

Let its vines
climb up winding lines
and sprawl over walls
like waterfalls

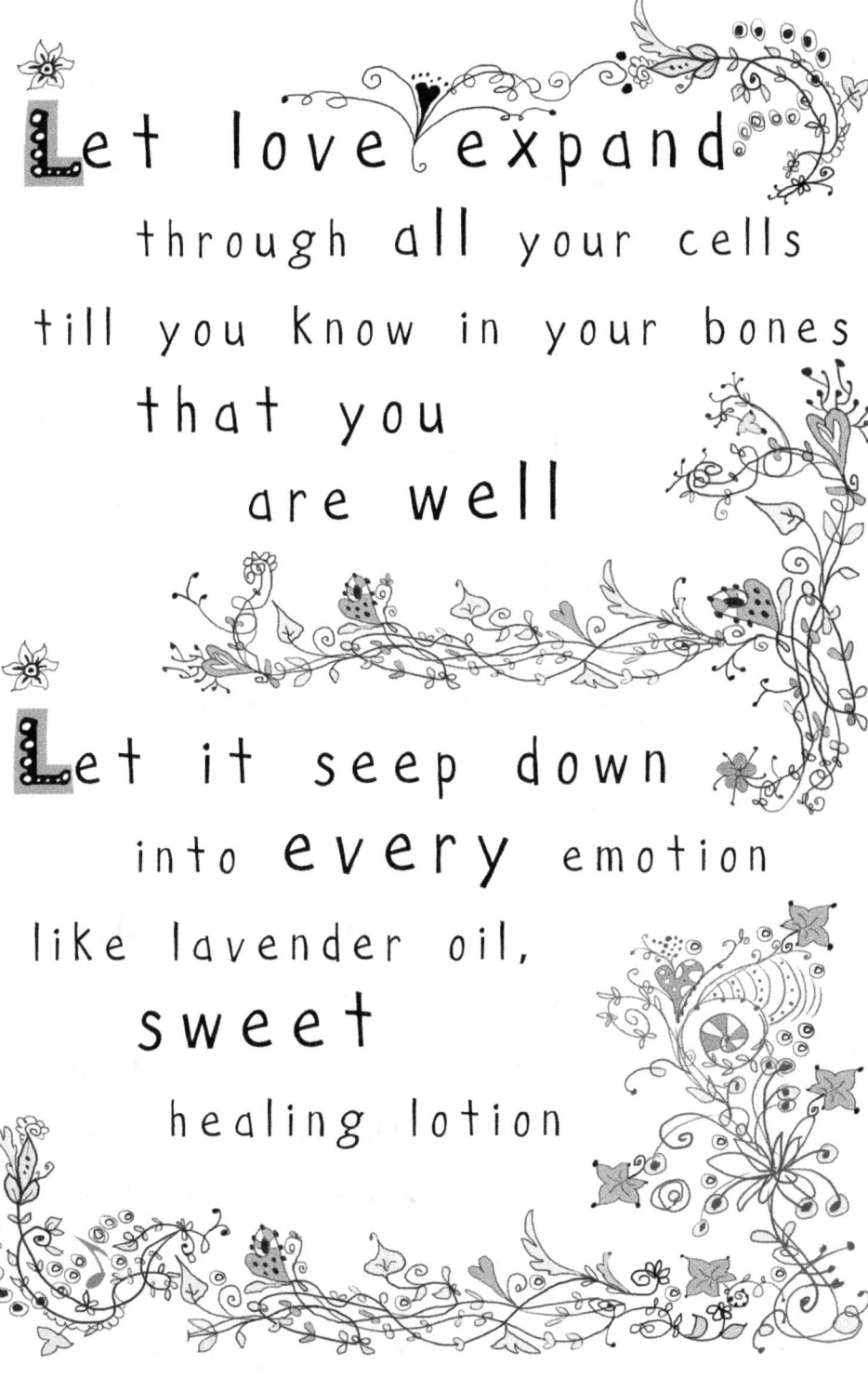

Let love expand
through all your cells
till you know in your bones
that you
are well

Let it seep down
into every emotion
like lavender oil,
sweet
healing lotion

Kelly Athena

Let it grow
from the heart
like a work of art
Be a leading guide,
a living chart
Let it urge you ahead
in forward motion
in ever expanding
upward promotion

Let love propel you
to take the leap
over unmapped waters
once thought too deep
To new horizons
and far flung places
To empty yet vibrant
galactic spaces

Let it
flow **down**
through your
darkest abyss
till you **know**
there is so
much **more**
than **this**

Let love
grow

Kelly Athena

MERMAID

I think I would feel good

if I could scuba in Aruba

like a mermaid underwater

like King Neptune's only daughter

I could swim fast like an otter

I would skim past like a yachter

I'd be long, tanned and trim

in fact a synonym with *joy*

If I would just act on my whim

and get out of here

Oh, boy!

MIRRORS

Everyone th[at] in my life
what annoys
actually stems
from something I see
that is the same
inside of me

I need to reframe
remove the blame
and take a look at me

Everyone that appears
in my life is a mirror
what annoys me about them
actually stems
from something I see
that is the same
inside of me

I need to reframe
remove the blame
and take a look at me

Kelly Athena

Wild Dancing Heart

MY AGENDA

Today my agenda is to
do nothing at all
except to watch patterns
of shadows
and light play on my wall
to wear my warm, soft bathrobe
all day
to wait for the sun to shine
on the leaves
outside my window
to wander between
worlds in my mind
and eat waffles
for dinner

Kelly Athena

PERCEPTION

Each event
that "happens to you"
seems like
a jagged shard
stabbing right through
your sense of
"how things should be"
in disjointed,
disappointing disarray
Blunder after blunder

Seen
by wise eyes
the same event
is perceived
as part of
an intricate pattern
an interplay
of light
and
dark
unfolding
in momentum
wonder after wonder

Kelly Athena

Kelly Athena

Question for a Cherry Tree

I asked the cherry tree,
"Have you **arrived**
when **spring**
is finally here,
you're green and new?
now have you
become **aware**?

Or have you **arrived**
when you have blossomed
in a **fanfare** of petals,
declaring your victory
over the cold?

Kelly Athena

Or is it when your flowers
have grown into juicy ripe fruit
held high by your branches,
ready to share?
Or could it be
when the cycle is done,
the fruit is picked,
and there's nothing to spare?
Is it when your twigs,
all gray and bare,
clatter in a game of solitaire
while you bask underground,
laughing, prepared,
waiting for spring
to come around?"

The cherry tree answered, "Life is simply doing what comes next. Just in being alive, you have arrived."

Kelly Athena

I'm watching her
in a distant mirror
From this view her life
seems clearer
I think I get the picture now

I don't need to worry how
to change or fix her

Accepting her
is the elixir

Kelly Athena

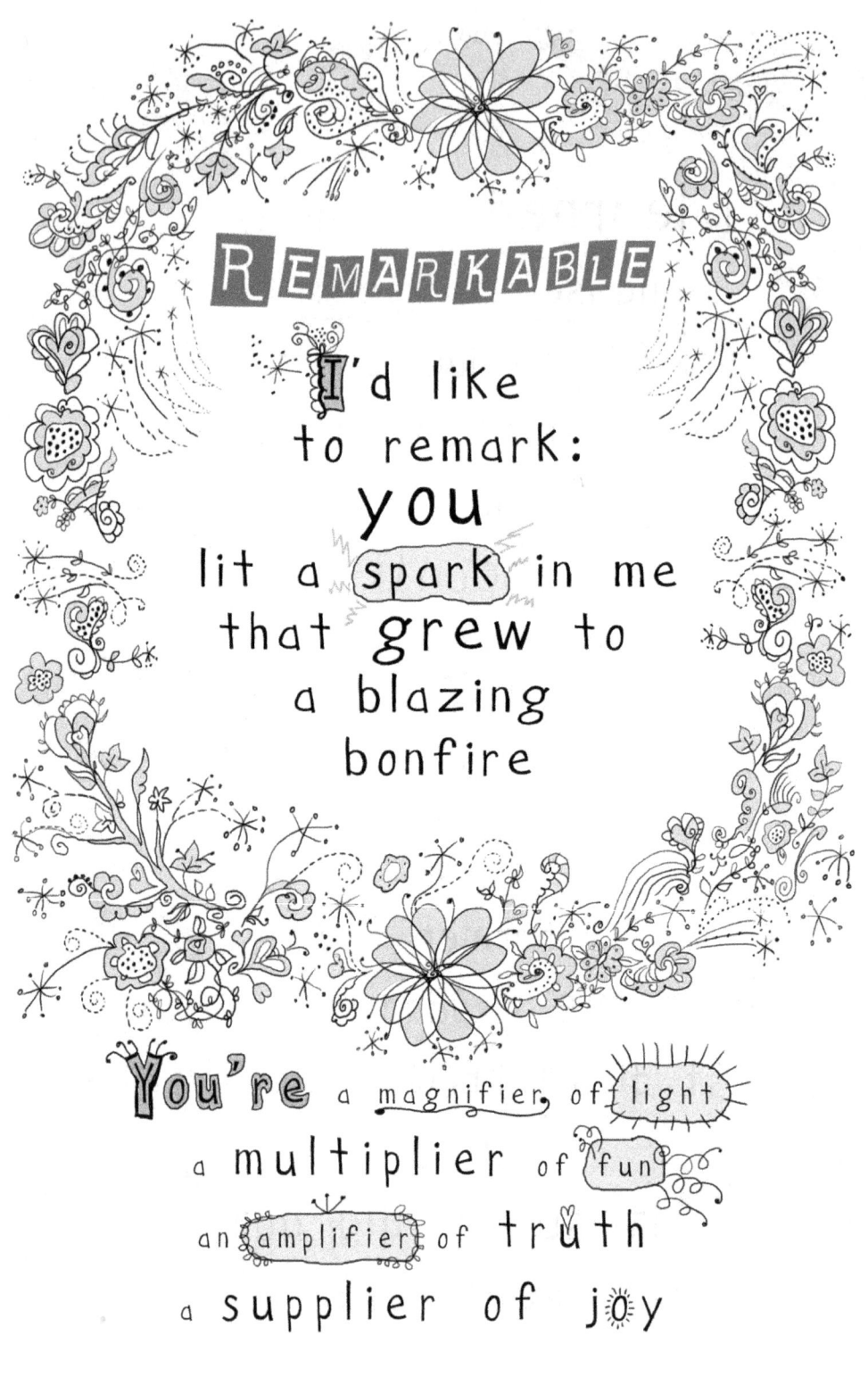

REMARKABLE

I'd like
to remark:
you
lit a (spark) in me
that grew to
a blazing
bonfire

You're a magnifier of light
a multiplier of fun
an amplifier of truth
a supplier of joy

This entire galaxy is inspired
by the things you (say)
You sway and sashay
to the beat of the universe

You're the gateway
to (fun)
the gourmet
of yum
You intersperse my day
with (exotic) spice

I interpret (you)
as a bright
juicy slice
of (paradise)

Kelly Athena

Right Now

There's nothing to get to.

You've already got it.

Oh, what shall I do
when the breakers curl
and rake me up
like a little pearl

Shall I stay unencumbered,
all unpacked?
so vulnerable
open to attack

Shall I find a new shelter
to hold me tight?
or just skinny dip
floating free
and light

Kelly Athena

soul scribbles

As I let my soul scribble
I see the truth drip out
little by little
I stretch out farther
toward the light,
fiddle and ramble,
sketch and doodle,
stumble and scratch
through doubt and fear
I shovel through piles
of grandiose guilt
things start to get clear
I regain my sight

Wild Dancing Heart

Spilling Out

My life is NOT cut and dried
like well-planned avenues and streets
↑ north and south ↓
straight up and down
→ east and west ←
in black and white
easy to navigate
like a grid on a map

No,

I spill out over the lid
like red wine
on a white linen tablecloth
of "supposed tos"
and "shoulds"

I snake out
in "S" curves and switchbacks
like a mountain stream
careening
through forests and meadows
scrambling
through thickets of undergrowth
saturating deep roots

Kelly Athena

spraying out soft mists
on spring blossoms
zigzagging
over rocks and boulders
splashing
across fences and borders
roaring into white cascades
plunging off cliffs into
unsupported
unknown
unattached
air
free falling

till something
    finally catches me far below
a granite bowl
    and then lets me go again

I freeze over
    in the middle of winter
I dwindle to a small, stagnant pond
    for a little while in between rains

I smile more
    since I quit resisting
the push and pull

        Yes, I'm spilling out
            and still I'm full

Kelly Athena

SPUN

Bury
the guns
Throw down
the swords
For we
are all spun
from the very
same
cord

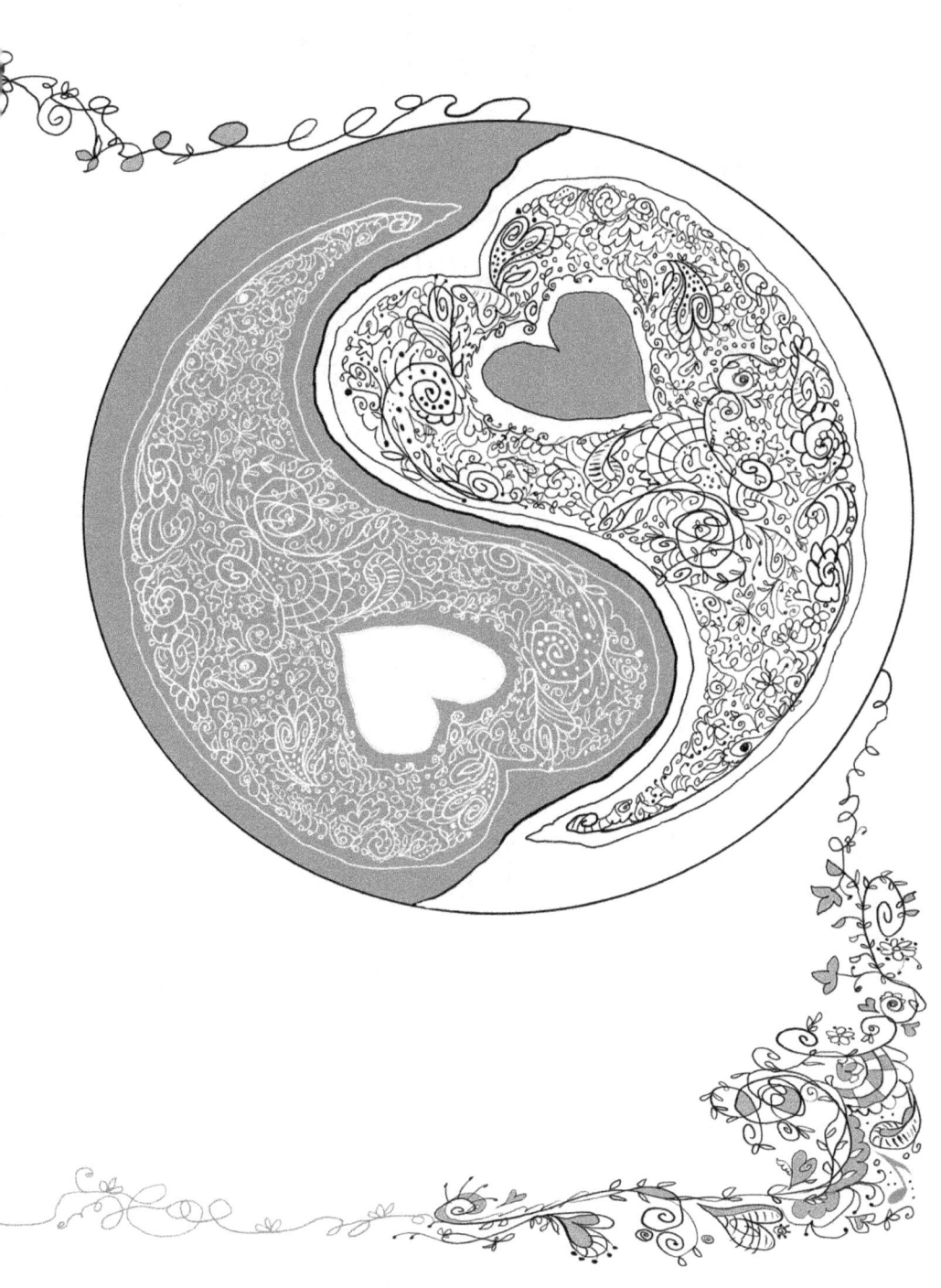

Kelly Athena

Star-Child

I eat stars for breakfast
I devour wandering planets
for lunch
I savor stray meteorites
for snacks in between

Crunchy sticks of light
Penetrating orbs of desire
Burning down my throat
I swallow them whole

Sizzling spheres
   slide down inside me
      revealing layers of luminescence
   right up to
         the edges of my **soul**

Every crevice and crack
      is **kindled** scorching
         breaking out in blazing fires

I smack my lips and feel flames
   spark and flash on my tongue

My favorite is Orion's belt buckle
   his very **belly button**
      That is the most
         delicious cluster of stars
            I have **ever** tasted by far

Kelly Athena

Once I descended from him
in an arching streak to earth
I could see everything
there was to see — what a trip!

Was it worth that glorious flight
to crash into gravity and slip into
flesh for awhile?

Why not?
I'll gleam here for a time
I sense a smile sneak up the sides
of my starry lips

I clap my hands
and let the stardust shake out
I watch the light launch
out of my fingers into colorful phrases
and surprising shapes

Book fairies flap their glittery wings
Twitterbugs twinkle
and whisper me things

They never sleep
They fill me
with flickering flames all night
till morning comes
and I pour myself out
with no hesitation
like the sun pours herself
into the sky
without reservation
and no need to ask why

Kelly Athena

SUCCESS

Success is **not measured**
by how **much** you've earned
but by how much **wisdom**
you have learned

Success is **not judged**
by what you've been granted
It's how many seeds
you've tenderly planted

Success is **not** how many
things you obtain
but how you **embrace**
and transform your pain

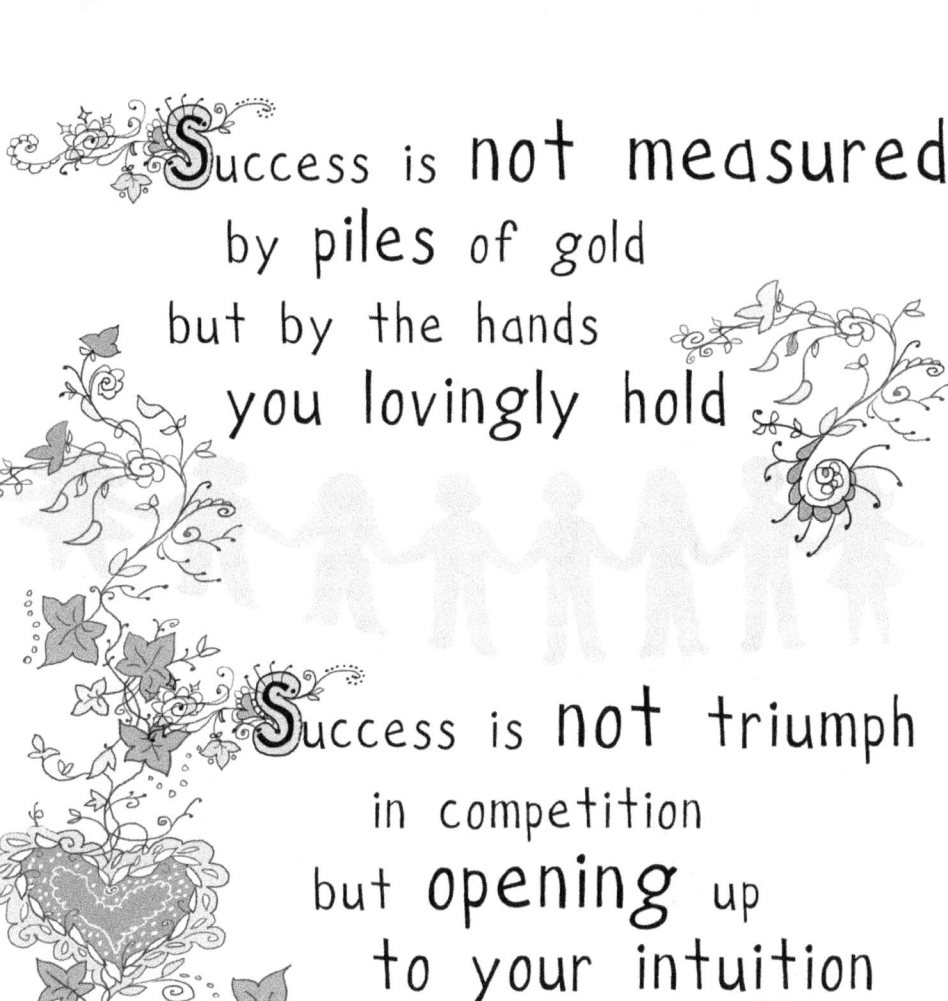

Success is **not measured**
by piles of gold
but by the hands
you lovingly hold

Success is **not triumph**
in competition
but **opening** up
to your intuition

Success is **not** what
you lose or gain
but how much hope
you still contain

Kelly Athena

A burning
circle of light
surrounds me
bursting with
relentless
regenerating power
Nothing can penetrate
the boundless
magnificence
of its devouring
brightness

Kelly Athena

the power of friendship

Together
we are a powerful force
We steady each other to stay on course
We've dropped the victim mentality
and made good times our reality

We sometimes get upset and disagree,
but that's okay we both are free
to say and do what we feel is right
We hold on loosely, not too tight

You are my connection to a lighter place
A place of compassion,
forgiveness and grace

When I look in your eyes I see love, not lies
We're friends forever
that's no surprise!

Kelly Athena

THE POWER OF JOY

May it **unify** your inner voices
and be the reason for all your **choices**
May you hold it close without resistance
let it be the **point** of your existence

May it untie your knots of **mystery**
and **rewrite** your view of history
May it play like a symphony
in your ears
May its streams **wash away**
your stagnant fears

May it be the substance
of which you're made
May it be the reason
you get paid
May it be your
book, chapter, and verse
submerse you in laughter
and fill up your purse

Joy

May it reign supreme as your life's theme
boost your esteem and color your dreams
May your whole life be a rhapsody
with joy as your signature melody

Kelly Athena

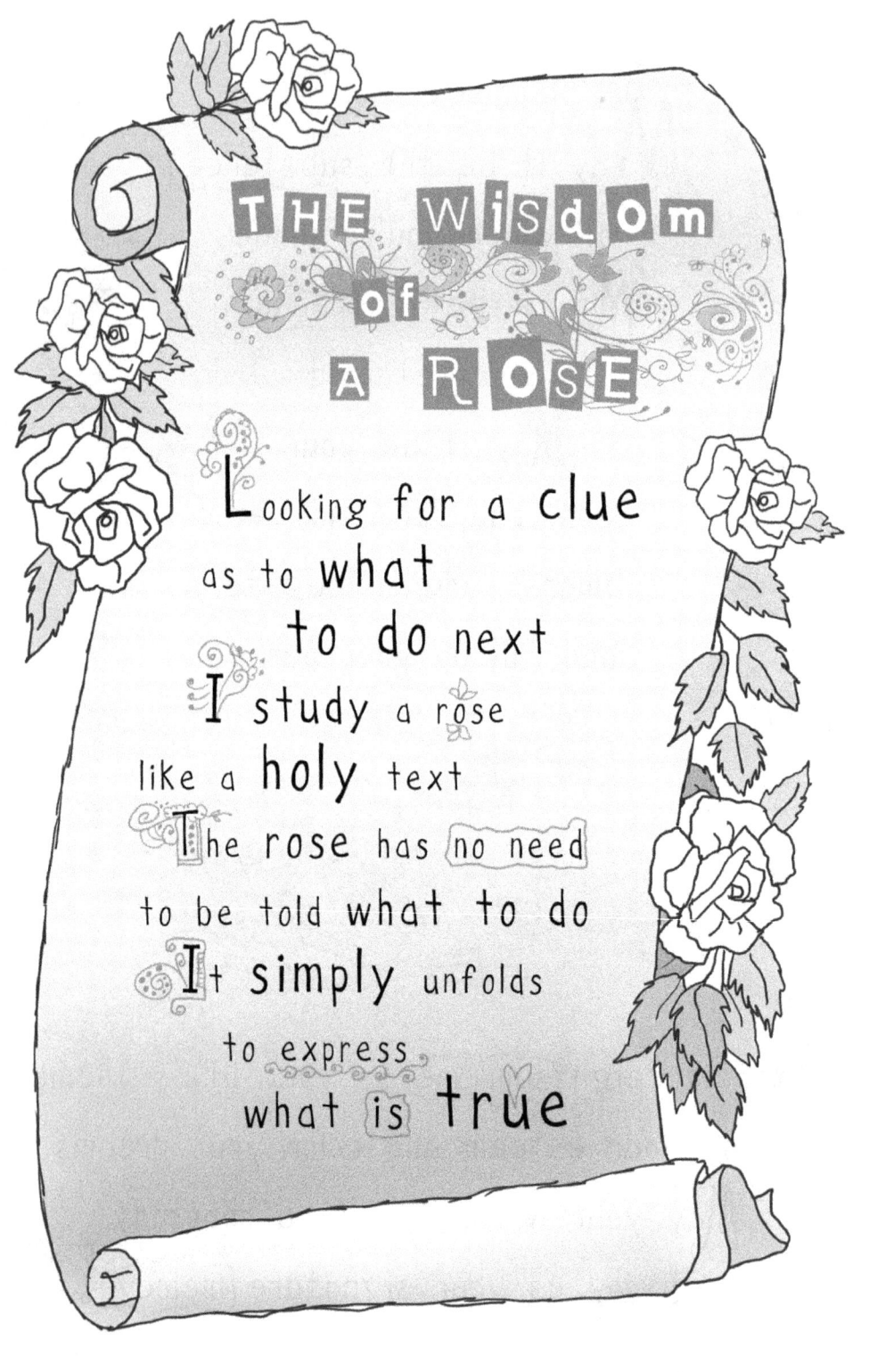

The Wisdom of a Rose

Looking for a clue
as to what
to do next
I study a rose
like a holy text
The rose has no need
to be told what to do
It simply unfolds
to express
what is true

In perfect geometry
it speaks to me
Its mathematical equation
needs little translation:
There is order
There is hope
There is love

Kelly Athena

To be a Bird

Little sparrows and finch
when caught
in a pinch

don't whine and moan
and ask, "Why me?"

who YOU are

Be
a red hot poker
or a **crazy** joker
Cry aloud
and beat
your hands
and feet
like
thundering drums
till morning comes

Wild Dancing Heart

Unwind the reel
of all you feel
Uncoil the snake
that's now awake
Breathe in and out
with
faith and doubt
Go fast, be still
burn hot, then chill

Search inside, outside,
near, and far
until you see who
you truly are:
through blinding dawn
and shrouded night
Now and Always
The Glorious Light

Kelly Athena

Thinking of how another should be robs me of my ability to be who I could be

Am I here to live my own life or another's?

Kelly Athena

Wild Dancing Heart

Wild Dancing Heart

My cells are alive
My quarks they wiggle
I jump and jive
I snort and giggle

I'm a dancing heart
wild and free
feeling a part
of life's potpourri

I may be quirky
I like to sway
I jitterbug
quiver and sashay

I'm a galaxy
My atoms squiggle
I'm full of hope
I'm all a-jiggle

Kelly Athena

you and me

There's nothing
not to Love
about you
You're lovely as
the morning dew

You're like a diamond
sparkling true
There's nothing not to Love
about you

There's nothing
not to Love
about me
I'm pretty as
a cherry tree

I'm flowing like
the deep blue sea
There's nothing
not to Love
about me

Kelly Athena

Wild Dancing Heart

Always **B**e **C**ertain:

Delightful **E**xperiences
will **F**ind you.
Go **H**eadlong
Into the **J**oyful
Kaleidoscope of **L**ife!
More **N**ow than ever before,
be **O**pen to the **P**ower
that **Q**uickens
your **R**adically **S**ensational,
Tremendously **U**ninhibited,
Vibrantly **Y**outhful
Zest!

Kelly Athena

happy Coloring and Sharing

Suggestion: Insert a thin
piece of cardboard behind
the page you are
coloring so the crayons, markers
or colored pencils won't leave
any markings on the
next page.

Kelly Athena

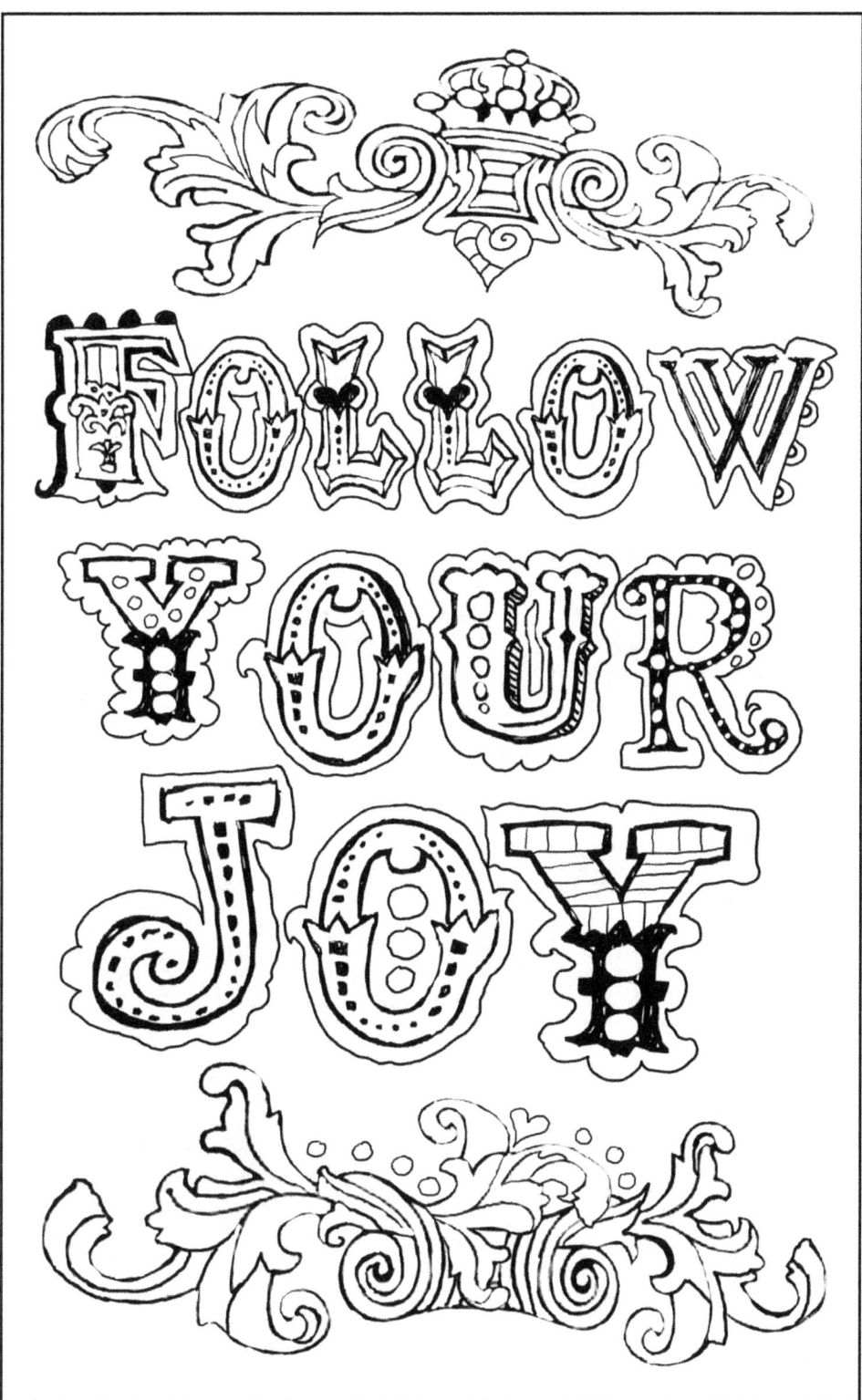

MORE ACTIVITIES FOR THE SOUL

Kelly Athena

Heart Puzzle

ACROSS
2 To open, as a flag (6)
5 Not trained (6)
7 Glide on the wind (4)
8 First 3 letters (4)
10 Hand digit (6)
11 Say I'll do something (7)
13 Metal piece that attracts (6)
15 Opens, as a map (7)
17 Deeply hear (6)
18 Aura, _____ worm (4)
20 Uplifting, enjoyable (10)
22 Basic class about numbers (12)
24 Zap of electricity (4)
25 Repeating shapes (8)
27 Deep happiness (3)

DOWN
1 Big creeks (7)
3 Distant locations (3, 5, 6)
4 Lion's sound (4)
6 Hugely, increasingly (13)
7 Personal destructiveness (4, 8)
9 Jail cubicles (5)
10 Concentrate, fixate (5)
12 Outer lemon peel; gusto (4)
14 Mind output (7)
16 Pollen collectors (4)
19 Hardwood tree (3)
21 Marriage vow (1, 2)
23 Dissolve, as a candle (4)
25 Frolic as a child (4)
26 After yesterday (5)

word search one

- ABCs
- Abused
- Abyss
- Agenda
- Angel
- Attic
- Bees
- Boundless
- Cells
- Certain
- Climb
- Corner
- Cry
- Dazzle
- Design
- Disjointed
- Doubt
- Dove
- Dream
- Elixir
- Emerge
- Emotion
- Equation
- Expand
- Explore
- Far-flung places
- Fear
- Fields
- Find
- Flutter
- Flying
- Focus
- Friendship
- Fun
- Gentle
- Glow
- Grid
- Growth
- Harsh
- Heartbeat
- Hope
- I do
- Intricate
- Jolt
- Joy
- Juice
- Jump
- Laugh
- Lavender oil
- Leaf
- Leap
- Let go
- Light
- Listen
- Magnet
- Melt
- Mountain
- Multitudes
- Nature
- Nest
- Now
- Oak
- Ocean
- Order
- Passion
- Peace
- Petals
- Play
- Possibilities
- Propel
- Quit
- Radical
- Roar
- Robust
- Roots
- Rule your world
- Saturating
- Savor
- Seeds
- Selfsabotage
- Soar
- Songs
- Spin
- Spun
- Surge
- Swirl
- Today
- Towns
- True
- Trust
- Unfolds
- Unfurl
- Uninhibited
- Unmapped
- Unsure
- Untame
- Vibrant
- Waterfall
- Wisdom
- Zest

Wild Dancing Heart

```
C D M M Y S U E D S L A V E N D E R O I L E S E N
J R U A T T I C E R J A U N F O L D S H G S R U T
H I L G P K I E I E E Q U A T I O N A R E O F F N
J P T N F Q B W X X F A Y G A D N E U L L H A T
F R I E N D S H I P W S M P H I T S D P V E A R E
B A T T S O I I T A I O E A M S R N X R T A R F A
L U U H E V Z A D N S N L S V J U E P A I F S L R
I Y D C L E U N E D D G T S I O E Z C D T O H U U
G U E E F U E N E P O S S I B I L I T I E S P N L
H N S R S G N E M N M Y A O R N R H W C M A I G E
T I Y T A B S S O A B Q Z N A T U R E A O V V P Y
F N B A B P O U U A P E U G N E M W I L T O T L O
L H J I O G I B N R U P P I T D O U B T I R E A U
U I U N T A M E T F E Q E M T L N E S T O G T C R
T B S E A N G H A K U G T D G N F C R T N S B E W
T I L T G R T W I U E R A B U S E D O A U H J S O
E T S A E W O B N P N I L P P E A C E R F W U W R
R E B M O N C C O R U D S A T U R A T I N G M K L
Z D E R F D E H E A R T B E A T F O C U S E P L D
F E G K I E A B C S O Y O B C Z G R A K C N R P J
I I Z C E S N R O O O M D Z E S O A R E T C R Y
D P N E L I X I R J U I C E A Z P B Z N L L X O G
O O Q D D G V G D F L Y I N G Y I U A O L E A P M
R A R I S N X G E C R G C T O W N S J V S J F E Q
A C K U W A T E R F A L L N F H N T N D A Z Z L E
```

Kelly Athena

word search two

Abyss
Angel
Attic
Bees
Blunder
Boundless
Butterflies
Cells
Change
Climb
Cobweb
Corner
Cry
Decline
Design
Disjointed
Doubt
Dove
Dream
Emerge
Expand
Fear
Fields
Fierce
Find
Flying
Focus
Freedom
Fun
Gardens
Gentle
Glow
Grid
Grow

Harsh
Heart
Honor
Hope
Ignite
Jagged shard
Jolt
Joy
Juice
Jumbled
Jump
Kindness
Laugh
Leaf
Leap
Let go
Light
Magnet
Melt
Mirror
Nest
Now
Oak
Ocean
Order
Passion
Peace
Play
Polite

Power
Propel
Quit
Roar
Roots
Rust
Savor
Seeds
Shelter
Soar
Songs
Spaces
Spin
Spun
Streams
Strong
Surge
Swirl
Taskmasker

Thought
Today
Tongue
Towns
True
Understanding
Unfolds
Unfurl
Unsure
Unwind
Waffles
Wander
Wisdom
Wonder

Wild Dancing Heart 148

```
W O N D E R S B Y D A X B X N S U R G E I O C
X F N R E E S O E R N G J U I C E M X H O P E
A I A D G D J U S E P W R A W A F F L E S T L
F E R N L F O N H A S T M I G U N F U R L Q L
F O A O L D L D E M V H I C D G A R D E N S S
O H F P N E T L L I P O R D O V E E M O F S P
C N M I B C P E T O O U R O T N Q D O C E A N
U H W A B L E S E S W G O P R O A K S N D F F
S N P C G I A S R P E H R O O E W R D H O I R
U Q A D F N C U N U R T C M T L S N V B A E E
V U S I L E E H J N N S W I R L I W S O A R E
D I S J O I N T E D S D N R H K N T I O V C D
J T I P R O P E L B P G E M E R G E E S A E O
T C O M G C L I M B I D D R B H A R S H D F M
A R N K T T I V A S N E S S S D O U B T A O L
S O U S N S G E E U L D E S A T T I C E S U M
K A U E S N H D L B L C M T O D A Y L S E H U
M R G Y I H T B M E A A B N A T O N G U E E N
A P B Y G H E U I P E X P A N D H N D L D A S
S A L U T W J F S R G L E T G O O G O I S R U
K F A A B B U T T E R F L I E S N L Z W N T R
E L U O Y L M S T R O N G W L R O O T S R G E
R U C N E O P C R Y W A N D E R R W G M N O W
```

Kelly Athena

Wild Dancing Heart

answers to heart puzzle

word search one
answers

```
C D M M Y S U E D S L A V E N D E R O I L E S E N
J R U A T T I C E R I A U N F O L D S H G S R U T
H I L G P K I E I E E Q U A T I O N A R E O F F N
J P T N F Q B W X X F A Y G A D N E U L L H A T E
F R I E N D S H I P W S M P H I T S D P V E A R A
B A T T S O I I T A I O E A M S R N X R T A R S R
L U Y U H E V Z A D N S N L S V J U E P A I F S H
I D D C L E U N E D D G T S I O E Z C D T O H U F
G U E E F U E N E P O S S I B I L I T I E S P R L
H N S R T S G N E M N M Y A O R N R H W C M A I U
T I Y T A B S S O A B Q Z N A T U R E A O V V P Y
F N B A B P O U U A P E U G N E M W I L T O T O L
L H J I O G I B N R U P P I T D O U B T I R E A U
U I U N T A M E T F E Q E M T L N E S T O G T C R
T B S E A N G H A K U G T D G N F C R T N S B E W
T I L T G R T W I U E R A B U S E D O A U H J S O
E T S A E W O B N P N I L P P E A C E R F W U W R
R E B M O N C C O R U D S A T U R A T I N G M K L
Z D E R F D E H E A R T B E A T F O C U S E P L D
F E G K I E A B C S O Y O B C Z G R A K C N R P J
I I Z C E S N R O O O M D Z E S O A R E T C R Y
D P N E L I X I R J U I C E A Z P B Z N L L X O G
O O Q D D G V G D F L Y I N G Y I U A O L E A P M
R A R I S N X G E C R G C T O W N S J V S J F E Q
A C K U W A T E R F A L L N F H N T N D A Z Z L E
```

Kelly Athena

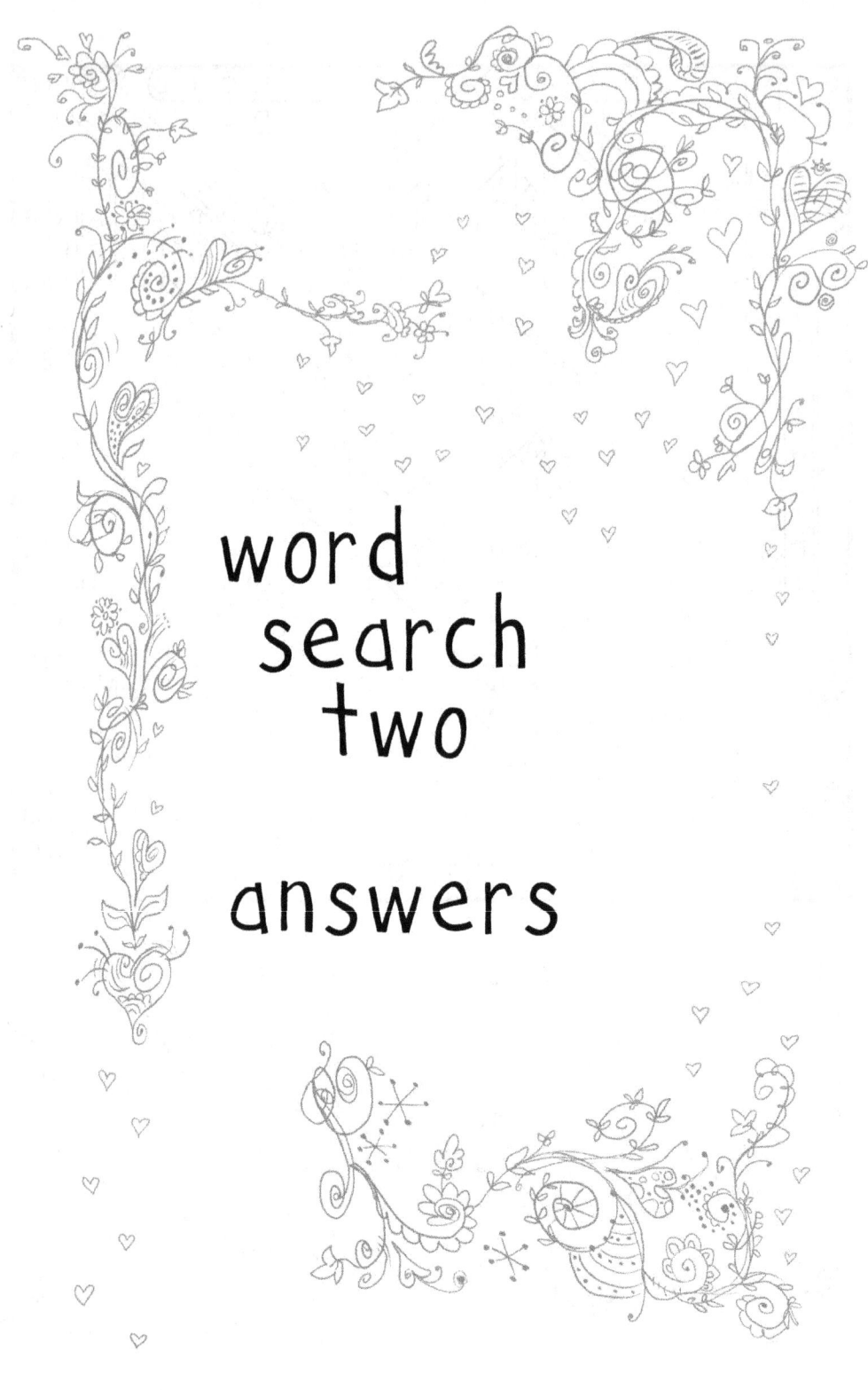

word search two

answers

```
W O N D E R S B Y D A X B X N S U R G E I O C
X F N R E E S O E R N G J U I C E M X H O P E
A I A D G D J U S E P W R A W A F F L E S T L
F E R N L F O N H A S T M I G U N F U R L Q L
F O A O L D L D E M V H I C D G A R D E N S S
O H F P N E T L L I P O R D O V E E M O F S P
C N M I B C P E T O O U R O T N Q D O C E A N
U H W A B L E S E S W G O P R O A K S N D F F
S N P C G I A S R P E H R O O E W R D H O I R
U Q A D F N C U N U R T C M T L S N V B A E E
V U S I L E E H J N N S W I R L I M S O A R E
D I S J O I N T E D S D N R H K N T I O V C D
J T I P R O P E L B P G E M E R G E E S A E O
T C O M G C L I M B I D D R B H A R S H D F M
A R N K T T I V A S N E S S D O U B T A O L
S O U S N S G E E U L D E S A T T I C E S U M
K A U E S N H D L B L C M T O D A Y L S E H U
M R G Y I H T B M E A A B N A T O N G U E N S
A P R Y G H E U I P E X P A N D H N D L D A R
S A L U T W J F S R G L E T G O O G O I S R U
K F A A B U T T E R F L I E S N L Z W N T R
E L U O Y L M S T R O N G W L R O O T S R G E
R U C N E O P C R Y W A N D E R R W G M N O W
```

Kelly Athena

getting deeper

play

explore

discover

Alphabet of Appreciation:

Write some things you are really grateful for that start with each letter of the alphabet. Come back later and add more words.

A

B

C

D

E

F

G

H

I

J

K

L

M
N
O
P
Q
R
S
T
U
V
W
X
Y
Z

Kelly Athena

Wise Letter:

Write a caring letter from your Wise Self to your Worried Self. Feel what it's like to BE your wisest self, connected to all compassion, truth, and power.

Dear Self,

I love you and want the best for you . . .

Liar, Liar, Pants on Fire:

What does your inner critic have to say about you and your creative plans? Write in pencil because you can erase these falsehoods anytime you want! Draw your inner critic, too.

Your Inner Friend:

What do you have to say to your inner critic? You have many inner friends and allies, aspects of yourself that are kind, resilient, persistent, and compassionate. Write down what they have to say in big letters with bold, bright markers. This is important stuff! Draw your inner friends. You may be surprised by your inner support group!

Meet The Author

Kelly Athena

Kelly Athena, M.A., is an award-winning poet who has taught creative workshops and college classes for thirty years. She encourages us to stay open-hearted, emphasizing that we can choose a new perspective each moment.

A Master Gardener, she loves learning about permaculture and sustainability. She is a pianist, composer, and past president of the County Arts Council. An avid bird watcher, hiker, and scuba diver, she is awed by the wonder of nature. A Master of Photography, she served as past president of the Phoenix Professional Photographer's Association and was named Arizona Photographer of the Year.

Growing up in the lush landscape of Northern California, her father inspired her with his passion for birds, flowers, gardening, and classical music. Her mother encouraged her creativity, hard work, love of jazz and jitterbugging.

She has also lived in Utah, Texas, Mexico, and Iowa. She now lives on the edge of the wild, howling Sonoran Desert in the foothills of Phoenix with her two cats and a small worm farm.

Look for Kelly Athena's next book in the upcoming year.

For more information, please visit KellyAthena.com.

Other Works by Kelly Athena

Literary:

How to Feel Good
2013

Discography:

Jazzy Birthday
26 upbeat instrumental compositions and arrangements

Bliss
One hour of meditative ambient music

Single Song Releases--Vocals and Keyboard

"*Amazing*"
Women's empowerment theme song

"*Dumpster Divin' Blues*"
A blues song about food waste and rescue

"*Queen of Hearts*"
Tribute song to Princess Diana
and other loving women

Meet The Artist

Lee Kaster

Lee Kaster grew up in Brooklyn, New York, a bike ride away from Coney Island, the location of the iconic beach boardwalk and amusement park of the 1950's. Her father was a watchmaker, portrait artist and photographer. Her mother was a painter who frequently took classes in Greenwich Village. Both parents were also Holocaust survivors which filled Lee with a deep gratitude for life. Lee dabbled with her mother's paints and loved observing her father work with intricate precision on watches and clocks. Lee was accepted into the High School of Art & Design in Manhattan, which quickly prepared her for the commercial art field. She went on to Pratt Institute where she majored in illustration and design. She won awards from the New York Historical Society, the Denver Advertising Federation and the Society of Illustrators. Her work was published by major publishers such as Harper Collins, Random House, McGraw-Hill, as well as greeting card companies and advertising agencies.

Lee began yearning for more creative personal expression and began experimenting with abstract painting and figurative sculpture. She moved to Denver where she maintained working relationships with her New York clients. The newly emerging abstract painter also started displaying her work at galleries and commissions followed. In the 1990's she quickly caught on to the digital revolution and applied it to her illustrations. She enjoyed Denver, but wanted a warmer climate so she adventurously packed up her Honda and drove to Scottsdale, Arizona, not knowing anyone there. She continued exploring her own artistic voice through abstract art. She also began teaching art as well as exhibiting. To Lee, design is the core of all art and life at the most fundamental level. The arrangement and composition of elements is the very basis of her teachings. Among Lee's numerous clients are the Phoenix Children's Hospital, Wells Fargo, Intel, Microsoft, JC Penney, Mayo Clinic and Toyota.

Kelly Athena

Inner Child

Kelly
the author

Notes

Notes

Notes

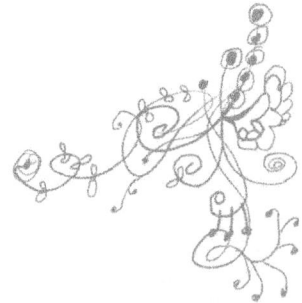

www.ingramcontent.com/pod-product-compliance
Lightning Source LLC
Chambersburg PA
CBHW061943070426
42450CB00007BA/1030